A Just Right Book

Richard Scarry's
Just Right
Word
Book!

Random House  New York

It is morning. The sun is up.
Brother Bunny gets out of bed.

curtain

window

pillow

blanket

bed

bathrobe

toy

bug

rug

slippers

block

Brother Bunny brushes his teeth.
Sister Bunny washes her face.

toothpaste

toothbrush

mirror

pajamas

faucet

sink

towel

nightgown

powder

shampoo

comb

brush

soap

glass

Brother and Sister Bunny
get dressed.
What should they put on?

boy

underwear

shirt

sweater

pants

cap

raincoat

sneakers

socks

boots

jacket

blouse

girl

underwear

dress

jumper

hat

mittens

socks

shoes

It's time to play.
What is everybody doing?

tail

kite

string

shovel

sand

pail

sandbox

roller skates

doll

wagon

jump rope

ladder

slide

ball

handlebars

friend

tricycle

wheel

sun

chimney

roof

window

bathroom

lamp

son

father

door

hall

living room

stairs

grass

The Bunny family
lives here.
What a nice house!

picture

bedroom

floor

bed

clock

garage

daughter

mother

wall

stove

sink

car

kitchen

driveway

bananas

grocer

scale

lemons

apples

oranges

raspberries

grapefrui

pears

melons

strawberries

blueberries

cherries

watermelon

grapes

peaches

pineapple

plums

shopper

cart

Mommy Bunny is buying groceries.
Where is Lowly Worm?

corn

lettuce

beans

peas

potatoes

pickles

tomatoes

beets

carrots

cucumbers

radishes

squash

cabbage

onions

turnip

cash register

milk

bread

can

pumpkin

eggs

bag

helmet

firefighter

nozzle

fire engine

passengers

SCHOOL BUS

school bus

bumper

dirt

hood

TAXI

taxi

car

antenna

bell

light

This is a busy street in Busytown.
The Bunny family is out for a drive.

driver

police officer

pencil car

motorcycle

street

dump truck

wheel

mail truck

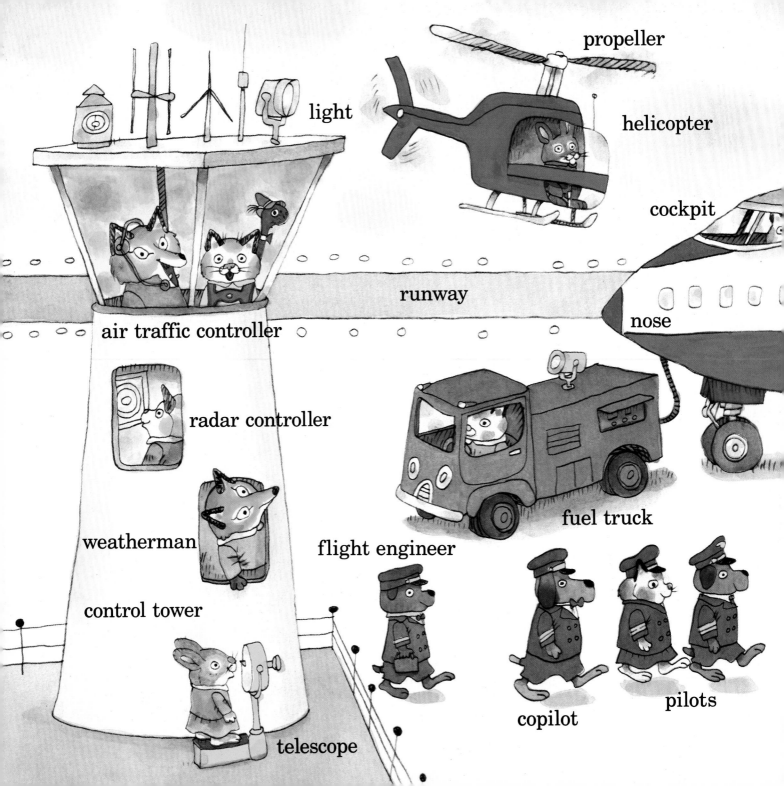

propeller

light

helicopter

cockpit

runway

nose

air traffic controller

radar controller

fuel truck

weatherman

flight engineer

control tower

copilot

pilots

telescope

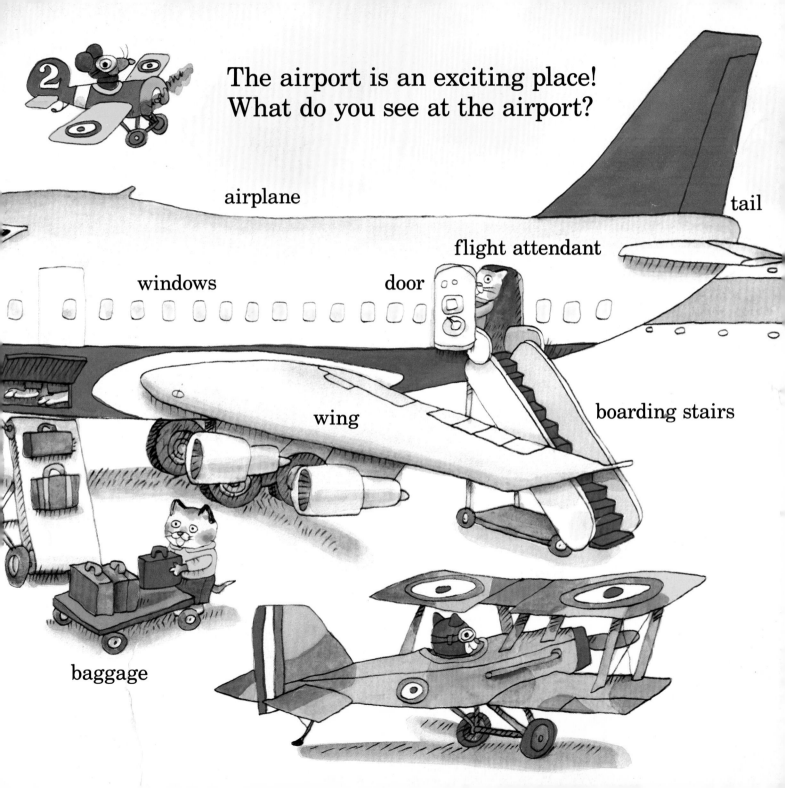

The airport is an exciting place! What do you see at the airport?

airplane

tail

flight attendant

windows

door

boarding stairs

wing

baggage

What a busy harbor!
Wake up, Fisherman Pig.

sail

lighthouse

sailboat

tugboat

pier

buoy

life preserver

passengers

FERRY

ferryboat

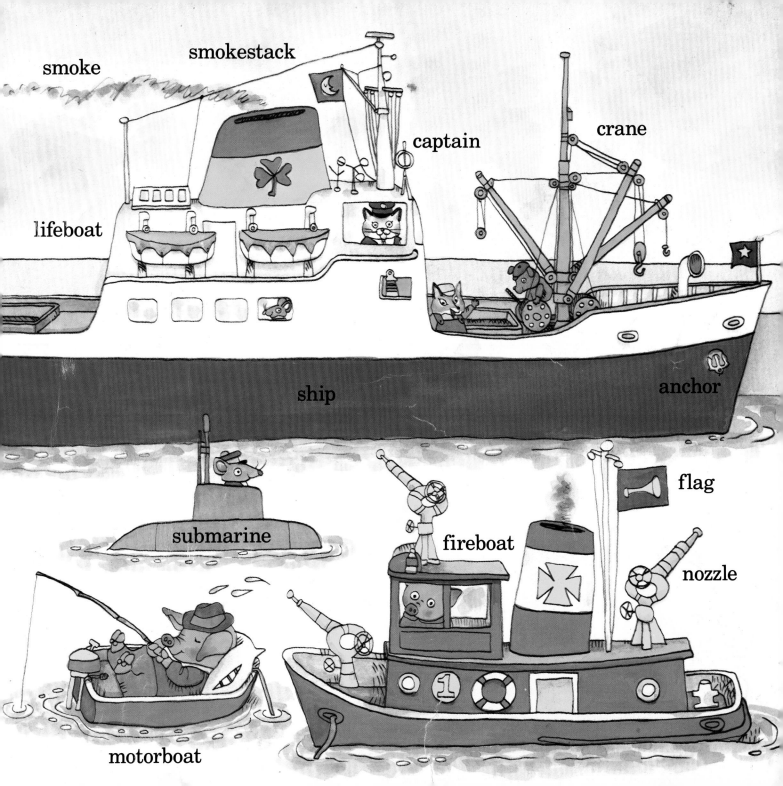

There's work for everyone on the farm. Who is guarding the corn?

corn

scarecrow

plow

tractor

weathervane

barn

windmil

hoe scythe rake pitchfork ladder sack barrel wheelbarrow